RENNA NIGHTINGALE

Hack Your Acting Audition

Fight the Battle Before, Own the Casting Room During, and Manage Your Mindset After the Audition, to Book Your Dream Roles

Headshots by Leah Huebner, Huebner Headshots.

First edition

This book was professionally typeset on Reedsy.
Find out more at reedsy.com

Contents

1

Your Story Starts Here

You've got a dream. You have an aching echo in your soul begging you to tell stories that move, inspire, and delight others because it's what you were wired to do! You know that if you were just given the chance, you could bring the house down! But, when you *are* given the opportunity to get into the audition room, the following mind loop is set into motion:

- "I have an audition! Yay!"
- "I have an audition. Oh crap."
- You work on the audition material. "I'm a genius!"
- You work on the material more. "I suck!"
- You show up to the audition. Everyone looks like you! And they all know each other! PLUS, they're bragging (LOUDLY) about having worked for the creative team before! You feel yourself beginning to shrink.
- You're next. Your palms are sweating.
- You're called into the audition room! Time magically slows down, while somehow also speeding up.
- All you can focus on is how you can't remember how to be a

human. WHAT do normal people do with their arms?!
- You start the material. You can't help but hear yourself as if for the first time. WHY did I make that acting choice?! What is the casting director thinking? Don't look at my resume, look at me, look at me, look at me!
- The audition is over.
- The mind games begin: "I crushed it! Or on second thought.... I tanked it."
- You overthink everything and can't decide how it actually went!
- This weighs on you heavily because if you don't get a callback, is it a sign you shouldn't even act anymore?!
- The confusion circles you like water in the drain until... your next audition. Rinse and repeat.

Does any of that sound familiar?

I've been a professional actor since I was eight years old. I just turned 30 (WILD!), and therefore I can confidently say I have spent well over TWENTY years of my young life ("young" is debatable at this point!) dedicated to perfecting the craft of auditioning. I've worked internationally as a lead vocalist and actor for some of the largest entertainment corporations in the world, on land and on sea. I've performed in over 100 regional stage productions across California. You've seen my face on the big screen, in your living room, and on your phone.

Here's what I've learned: *the audition is so much more than just an audition.* It's a chapter in your story, a dare for you to be bold and courageous, an inciting incident for you to push through what you thought you were capable of. It's the next step to becoming the artist and human you were meant to be.

And THERE lies freedom.

What to Expect

I'm a type A, color-coded-pens, detailed note-taker kind of gal. If you also identify as a Hermione Granger of sorts, this is for you:

In section one, I am going to show you how to Jedi-master the HECK out of audition prep. Because here's another secret: if you smash this part of the process, 95% of the battle is fought before your audition. *Wouldn't you love to walk into the room knowing you've already won?*

Next, we'll talk about how to own the casting room during your audition. This is where we are going to enlist our brains, hearts, and lungs to play on the same team so that nerves, fear, and anxiety have "no power here!", as Glinda the Good says to the Wicked Witch. When employing these new skills, you can empower yourself to be essentially fearless. *Auditioning will become a fun treat instead of a psychological terror.* Who's with me?!

Last, but not least, we are going to manage your mindset *after* your audition. Because, guess what? When the audition is over, it doesn't feel like the audition is actually over, does it? You're waiting to hear if you'll move onto the next step, and guess what else—this is your passion, so the audition experience is still living in your brain, rent-free. If left unmanaged, these potentially poisonous thought patterns can become your Achilles' heel and break you down before your next audition, leading to a vicious cycle of self-defeat. But not for you! YOU are taking charge of your audition process and together, *we will unlock your next step to freedom from post-audition mind games!*

What Not to Expect:

I am an actor and acting coach and therefore obsessed with acting theory and could literally nerd out all day about it. For the purposes of this book, I am focusing on the "how's" of preparing to crush your audition, how to bring your best and be present IN the audition, and your mindset after! For the depths of scene study and the art of acting, one hundred million percent, join an acting class and work with a reputable coach (there are many of us—if you think you and I would work well, see my email at the end!), and keep a look out for my next book to dive deeper into acting theory there!

Let's Fricken Do This

I am ridiculously passionate about empowering others to pursue their performing dreams. Auditioning has shaped who I am on a molecular level. It has made me brave, bold, vulnerable, tenacious, resilient, and creative. Auditioning is a wild thing and I have not so much learned how to tame it, but how to befriend it, and how to let it make me a stronger version of myself through process, patterns, and play.

By the end of this book, that's what you'll learn, too.

In the words of *Hamilton*, "Raise a glass to freedom!"

Sorry. Once a theatre nerd, always a theatre nerd.

Let's fricken do this.

2

Before the Audition, Part 1: Fighting the Mini Mind Games

Auditioning can be a minefield—or a "mind-field." Let me explain.

When mixing something we're passionate about (performing) with something high stakes (an audition), our brains can get needlessly nasty in 0 to .25 seconds!

Welcome to chapter 1, where we will equip you to undermine the "mind-field" before self-sabotage strikes.

Without further ado, let me be the Obi-Wan Kenobi to your Luke Skywalker. It's time to use The Force against those malicious mind games.

Auditions are Mini Mind Matches

We've all been guilty of not studying for a test, right? We knew the test was approaching, looming like a shadow in the dark. But, for whatever reason, we just couldn't bring ourselves to study. Maybe we were busy with other homework or auditions, or we just plain didn't want to study. We tossed the responsibility to the side with a cavalier, "It'll be fine."

Unfortunately, in my guilty case study, the test was NOT fine. On the morning of said test, I was a wreck. I was shaking! My shoulders were up to my ears, and I had a knot the size of Texas in my stomach. All of my nerves caused me to second-guess every answer on the test. The record player in my head scratched on: "You're going to fail!" Not a lovely refrain to hear over and over in your brain! When it comes to the grade I got on the test? You guessed it: I tanked it.

What happened here? I could have easily changed my entire experience by simply studying for the test. Instead, I didn't play the mind game well. I gave into procrastination and fear instead of taking charge of the situation. Neglecting to prepare led me to bullying myself, experiencing anxiety, and ultimately, failing.

Proper preparation is a toolbox overflowing with tactics we can use to avoid negative mind loops before, during, and after our auditions.

In life, negative thoughts are gonna be coming at you from all directions. Add an audition that could lead you closer to your dreams? The negativity is working overtime to knock you out. Fighting back against those thoughts can feel like a full-time job if you don't have the right tools.

Here are some preparation tools to help you defeat those mini

7

mind games.

Self-Talk:

Our primal desire to succeed can take a dangerous turn by manifesting in harmful self-talk if we're not prepared to whip that self-talk into fighting shape!

Here are just a few of the harmful things I've thought and said to myself during auditions:

- I hate the sound of my voice.
- I'll never be as captivating as she is.
- Why do I always make that weird face?
- I shouldn't have even tried.
- I'm embarrassing myself.
- Casting called me back out of pity.
- That was the worst performance I've ever given.
- I suck.
- Nobody wants me here.
- Just go home.

Do any of these sound familiar? If the answer is "yes," you're not alone. Let's be real: you're not *human* if you haven't experienced negative self-talk!

But negative self-talk isn't gonna fly anymore. *I never, ever, ever, want you to talk to yourself that way again!*

EVER!

You have to be your own best cheerleader. Shooting yourself down has never helped you to be better or stronger. From now on, you're your own best friend and fan. You are going to root for yourself even when no one else does! Your mind is going to be a fun, *safe* place for you to hang out, free of bullying and negativity!

There is no honor in being unkind to yourself.

Here's a good test: would you say that phrase to your 6-year-old self? No? Then cut it out! My best friend has started keeping a picture of her toddler self in her car to remind herself to steer away from negative-self talk. If she starts thinking something rude about herself, she is interrupted mid-mean thought by coming face to face with her younger self. In her words, "You just can't be mean to that sweet little girl!" Genius! Why don't you try making a younger photo of yourself your phone background? Or keeping a younger photo of little you in your wallet? This is a practical way to cut the hurtful chit chat!

Now, I'm not saying you shouldn't be accountable for your goals. There is a difference between setting boundaries for yourself and being harmful with your inner dialogue.

Set high expectations for yourself: Set goals like practicing your audition materials five times a week, reading scripts (instead of defaulting to playing video games or mindlessly scrolling through social media), taking classes, and watching YouTube videos from artists you admire about their process.

When you don't meet your goals, have a chat with yourself. Remind yourself what really matters to you and what is actually going to help move you toward the things you want. And then, give yourself grace to get up and try again.

The Power of Affirmations

What is the negative self-talk you hear on repeat in your head?

Is it, "I'm not good enough?" Or, "I don't belong here?" Or, "I'm a failure?"

Think of the phrase that taunts you the most, and instead of getting angry at yourself for hearing that nasty voice, I want you to create a counter affirmation.

Choose one of these:

- I am enough.
- I am here for a reason.
- I can figure anything out.
- I am capable.
- I am powerful.
- I am radiant.
- I am resilient.
- I am an artist.
- I am free and safe to create.
- I love myself for who I am.
- I was made for this.
- I deserve to chase my dreams.

Or, create your own affirmation and share it with me in an email!

It takes a while to reformat our thoughts, but it *absolutely* can be done! Start your day by repeating your affirmation(s) to yourself. When you notice that negative belief circulating in your head, observe it. And then decide to change course.

Our first thought is the way we have been conditioned to think. Our reaction to that thought—the new positive affirmation—is what we actually believe.

No longer accepting our first negative thoughts about ourselves is the way we will begin to replace toxic self-talk with positive thoughts that will move us toward freedom, peace, and joy within ourselves.

It's imperative to change your thought patterns to remind yourself over and over that freedom, peace, and joy are *exactly* what you deserve—especially in a world that often tells us the opposite.

Stay in Your Own Lane

Who here has been personally victimized by comparison?

Y'all better get BOTH hands in the air!

Auditions can be a feral breeding ground for toxic comparison, which is the next mini battle we are going to equip you to fight.

It's beyond natural to begin the comparison game when we are literally fighting for the same role! As performers, our minds and bodies are our instruments. It's not like we're accountants where we can separate our math from ourselves and turn in reports. Or, like painters, who use their hands but get to leave their art on their canvases. WE ARE THE CANVAS, BRO.

This triggers everything about the audition process to feel *far* more personal and send us down the yellow brick road of comparing... and let me tell you: there's no Emerald City waiting for us down that road!

Here are some ways to guard yourself when the big, bad comparison wolf comes a-knocking in your mind:

You are Unique:

It may sound cheesy, placating, and rather "Zen" of me, but for real: there has never been anyone created exactly like you in the history of the world.

Think about that.

There's never been a replica of you with your exact likes, dislikes, hobbies, taste buds, height, eye color, talents, fingerprints, humor, penchant for cute kitten videos, etc.

I don't care if you're standing shoulder to shoulder with someone who "looks exactly like you" in the audition room.

You are different and have unique gifts, strengths, and abilities. You would bring something totally different to the role.

Remember, auditions are untamable, subjective processes and not getting the role does not make someone "better" than you, but rather, they were better matched with the creative team's vision.

You are valuable, whole, and matchless exactly as you are.

The more confident you can become in your individuality as an artist, the less tempted you will be in waiting rooms to compare yourself to others!

How Would You Do It?

One of the best ways to fight comparison before it even darkens your door is to be thrilled about what you're bringing into the audition room.

How do we do that?

By bringing yourself to the material.

If you were in that situation, what would your honest reaction be? What do you? What do you find funny? Offensive? Delightful?

I always love to make at least one authentic and uniquely different choice in every scene. Something that shows my heart, personality, and something quirky I would bring to the piece.

Bringing my own unique choices to the material makes me downright giddy! I waltz into the audition room super smug because I feel so clever about my choice. I cannot wait to share it with the team in the room!

This keeps my focus from darting around me to the people I'm auditioning with, wondering what they have that I don't; and laser-focused on my material, and how excited I am to get in there and show it off!

Fight the Fear

If you ask a million people how they're feeling about their upcoming audition, 999,999 of them will say, "Nervous!"

Which is totally understandable! Hi, we're not making friend-ship bracelets here! We're exposing pieces of our soul! We're sharing shades of our passions with strangers who have the power to give us what we want or metaphorically toss us aside!

Um, yeah. Being nervous makes sense.

But, does it serve you?

That's a hard "no," Stan.

I've got some incredible tools for you in chapter two to physically fight any manifestations of nerves, but for this pre-audition focus, I want you to hone in on your language.

As we've seen, language matters.

It matters for your self-talk, and it also matters for your brain.

14

If you tell your brain that it's nervous, guess what? It will be. Let everyone else be nervous. You can make a different choice.

From now on, when asked about how you feel about your upcoming audition, here are four ways you're allowed to respond:

- Focused.
- Prepared.
- Excited.
- Ready.

Practice infusing yourself with confidence by using affirming terminology. It's a scientifically proven version of "Fake it 'til you make it."

Your language wires your brain. So don't tell yourself to be nervous! You are focused, prepared, excited, and ready.

Mic drop.

Wrap it Up:

You do not have to play along with the negative mind games associated with auditioning. You have the power to:

- Curate your self-talk into a litany of empowerment and inspiration!
- Cut out comparison by focusing on how you were uniquely

created, what YOU bring to the table, and being downright giddy to share what you've created in the room!
· Shut down fear by rewriting the language you use, and thus rewiring your brain.

Half of the pre-audition battle is mental. By employing these strategies, you will sky-rocket in confidence, fearlessness, and freedom.

Whoa—the force is strong with this one.

Steal These Affirmations from above:

- I am enough.
- I am here for a reason.
- I can figure anything out.
- I am capable.
- I am powerful.
- I am radiant.
- I am resilient.
- I am an artist.
- I am free and safe to create.
- I love myself for who I am.
- I was made for this.
- I deserve to chase my dreams.

3

Before the Audition Part 2: "The Tangibles" Pre-Audition Bootcamp

May I just say, you're doing great. You've picked up new skills to prepare your mind for the battles you'll face in the field! And now, we're getting a little less "meta." It's time to talk about the tangibles: the actions you're going to take to prepare you for your audition experience from the time you pull up outside the building, to then time you're calling your Mom to tell her how great it went afterwards.

Alright, y'all. Welcome to "The Tangibles" Pre-Audition Boot-camp.

Preparation

Listen, I get it. "Preparation" is not a particularly sexy word. It's not thrilling or spicy. But you know what it *is*? Game-changing.

Here is the (not yet!) patented Renna Nightingale definition of the word Preparation. Ahem:

Preparation (n.)

1. *Reducing the number of things that could throw you off in the audition room.*

2. *Maximizing the things that will help you take control, be creative, and ultimately, book.*

Please, hold your applause!

Let me break it down for you:

Preparation is the difference in your audition between:
   -making choices or being chained to your sides
   -presenting your "in-progress" or presenting something you're proud of.
   -walking in fear or walking in freedom.

I have spent most of my life in audition rooms, often being paired with other actors and getting to experience their processes firsthand. I have been an acting coach for many years. I have even been on the other side of the casting table. With a bajillion years (ok, twenty-two) of audition experience, here is something I have discovered to be absolutely true:

You do not have the freedom to play, be creative, bring your whole self to the project, or to do your best, without being prepared.

Here is what I mean by being prepared:

1. **You are memorized.**

Note: This rule applies when you are either bringing your own material to an audition, i.e. a monologue or a 16-bar-cut; or you are presenting sides you've been sent at least the day before.

Now, when I say "memorized," I don't mean that you've merely heard it before and you can pretty much get it right if you can kind of *glance* at it. No! This level of memorization does not hold up when you are nervous or under any kind of pressure (*ahem*, in an audition!).

To be truly memorized is to have your lines down *cold*. My acting professor used to say, "You're not ready for the audition unless you can do the entire scene without the script in Times Square at a crosswalk as millions of tourists try to pass you and the creepy Minnie Mouse takes her fake head off next to you." Or something like that.

The audition room can be full of distractions, and you've got to be so memorized, nothing can throw you off!

Here is a wild list of things that have *actually* happened while I was in the room (non-exhaustive):

-a cell phone rang
   -the reader read the wrong scene
   -the casting director (CD) checked their phone
   -the CD ate a Subway sandwich
   -the power went out
   -the creative panel was in a rush and started the scene the second I walked in
   -a dog barked

-the team started me halfway through the scene

-the air conditioning went on

-someone behind the casting table hacked up what sounded like a lung

-you could hear the singing audition next door

-you could see other actors watching from the window

-the CD gave me directions to take the scene in an entirely different direction

-someone fainted

Woof. If any of these things were to happen to you during your audition, could you keep going? If you knew the scene backward and forward, heck yes, you could!

The "main character" of this point, if you will, is to *take control* of your audition. I want you to master your material so thoroughly, it would take an apocalypse to derail you from doing your best. Copy?

Now, say it with me: *I will never walk into an audition room without memorizing my material again.*

Finally, if your audition requires you to bring in your own material, which, 99% of the time, is going to be a song or a monologue, the memorization rule applies DOUBLY. I'm not gonna lie. Forgetting the words to material you chose is a rookie move. Don't be that guy.

2. You've broken down the material.

In the thrill of the chase, sometimes we forget that we are not just competitive robots out for the kill. (Just me?)

It's tempting to lose sight of the fact that the thing that got us into storytelling in the first place, was the art of it.

When you initially get a script, your first role is that of a detective. Glean as much information as you possibly can to piece together this specific world you're stepping into. Here's what you do:

· Read the entirety of the sides.

Often, part of the script you're given will be crossed out, denoting you're not performing it in the room. I don't care that it's crossed out, and neither do you! Read every single thing on the page! Your role here is as an archaeologist, digging out the bones of the scene to comprehend the full story! (Yes, I know we've switched roles from actor to detective to archaeologist, but keep role-ing with me! Get it?)

· Research the project.

Is this a big-budget film? A musical? A web series? A remake? An indie? At the very least, give it a Google search to make sure you're bringing the right tone to your material.

Once you've figured out 1) what the project is, and 2) have grasped a clear understanding of what the scene is, now you can dive into your character.

· Who the Heck are You?

Is this one of your favorite parts of the process? It should be! You get to whip out your experience and creativity, and marry them into a brand-new character!

Just like you know all the details about yourself: your preferences, fears, hopes, dreams, favorite cereal, etc; you need to know everything about your character! For the sake of the audition, come up with enough ideas about who this person is to give a fleshed-out performance. Make sure your character has opinions about everything in the scene!

- Pinpoint what you're fighting for.

In every single scene and song, your character wants something and is actively trying to get it. THIS is what sets you apart. THIS is what keeps the material fresh for you. THIS is where the fun is, and where the magic is. The arc of the scene changes depending on who is reading with you and HOW they are reading with you. It's thrilling!

This is also the thing that prepares you the most for your audition. You are an actor! We have gone beyond the rudimentary level of regurgitating lines and lyrics. You are using the words as a tool to get what you want. The material is a part of you. The casting director is watching you become a storyteller with your own voice, opinions, thoughts, and unique spark.

When you know what you are trying to achieve with the material, you are ready to present your own authentic version of the story with casting. Can I get a "woot woot?!"

3. You've sung the song/ read the scene/ performed the monologue for someone else.

Here's a secret that has kept me afloat: *I never, ever, ever perform material in an audition without practicing it for someone else first.* In an emergency, this is my mom on FaceTime. Ideally, this is my coach.

Performing your material in front of another person is very different from performing your material by yourself in the mirror. There's an additional light bulb that flicks on in your brain—an awareness, a heightened level of reality when someone is watching you. So, I ALWAYS practice my new songs or scenes in front of another human first. It prepares my brain for the conditions it can expect in the audition.

Therefore, once again, I have controlled as much as I can to minimize the fear of the "unknowns."

I get it though—sometimes, performing your sides for someone else before the audition is unrealistic. You're at a callback and they give you new sides, or the audition is a cold-read (when you get a script on the spot!).

BUT, when you can, from now on, you ALWAYS will practice in front of another human! Got it? Good.

A special kick-ball-change note for MT auditions: ALWAYS make sure you hear the piano accompaniment of your song before you get into the room with a live pianist! Pop/ rock style shows are more and more the rage these days, and often, the piano version sounds NOTHING like the music you're used to. Without drums, guitar, bass, synth, etc; the pop song you knew like the back of your hand might as well have been translated into Zulu.

Find the piano version on YouTube, Spotify, iTunes, or hire someone to create a piano track for you!

A well-respected audition accompanist once confided in me, "People ask me all the time to play their audition song *in the room* before they start because they've never heard the accompaniment before!" That's not a super great first impression to make in front of casting, is it?

4. You have prepared backup material of your own.

You know what stresses me out most about auditions? Thinking, "What if they ask me for something else in the room?" Because oftentimes, they do!

What do we do to eliminate that stress altogether? Prepare a backup song or monologue.

This extra material should be a piece you love! It should be a delight to perform—something you feel amazing about and have already worked with a coach on. You could sing it in the rain, on a train, with a fox, in a box (You get it).

5. You've chosen what to wear.

Here are my tips as a female-identifying actor for what to wear, but regardless of your gender identity, let your ultimate goal with your audition outfit be this: to feel confident, and to *not* think about your outfit while you're auditioning. In other words, nothing about your outfit makes you feel uncomfortable or is distracting to you or casting.

To me, that equates to four things:

· Stable shoes.

Me walking in heels is rather like watching a baby lamb scramble for safety on ice. Not good. Platform heels and chunky boots are my friend when heels are required! I always want to feel grounded in the room! If you can feel grounded in stilettos, more power to you! But, one hundred percent of the time, the casting team would rather see you comfortable and focused in slightly less fabulous shoes, than your sickest pair of high heels! If you're going to a musical theatre audition, do not wear your character shoes to sing. It is considered unprofessional and screams, "First year of MT!" Just bring a good pair of heels to change into for the singing portion!

· Stable straps on top.

I once did a callback wearing an adorable dress that was too big in the shoulders. Every time I tried to move, my sleeves fell down! I was constantly pulling those suckers up! I don't even remember what I said or did in the scene. This is another reason why strapless dresses and tops are a "no go" for me. I'd rather be fighting for my objective in the scene than fighting with the sleeves of my dress! What a distraction!

25

- Comfortable length.

Listen, I love a short skirt or dress! Just not in the audition room, unless the character calls for it. If I get the urge to tug it down, automatically, it's too short for most auditions because it has officially distracted me from the work! If you're afraid of flashing the casting team, ditch it.

- Quiet jewelry.

Story time! I was called back for the lead in a brand-new Jason Robert Brown musical! Hallelujah! I wore an adorable cherry-print dress with a long, dangly hearts necklace. I felt like a 10/10... until I got word from my agent that Jason himself had asked me *not* to wear the necklace to my next callback...because it clanged so loudly! I've never worn the necklace since!

This applies to clinking earrings, tinkling necklacing, jingling bracelets...if it makes noise, tell it to join a band and you'll wear it after your audition.

General Notes

Now that we've got the basics down, it's time to think like your character.

If your project was set today, what would your character wear from your closet? If you've got a TV/ Film audition, plain colors with texture look great on camera. Too much of a print can be dizzying! Pro tip: take a quick video on your phone to check how your outfit will reads on screen!

If it's a theatre call, try to stay away from the jewel tone fit and flare dresses. It was the standard a few years ago, and several casting directors have said it's a quick way to appear "green," which means "new to the industry." I love tights and boots, so I'm often layering them under dresses or shorts because it's how I feel great! What's your style? How can it translate to your character?

The most important thing is always to feel comfortable, which boosts your confidence, and allows you to focus on the actual goods—your performance!

6. You've packed your audition bag.

For in-person film / TV auditions, I don't usually bring much: just water, a protein bar in case I end up waiting for a while, two copies of my headshot and resume (unless otherwise indicated—sometimes, it's all digital!), and some lip gloss if the character would.

It's a different story for MT auditions. Can I take a moment to wax poetic about my audition bag? It's bright yellow, which makes me happy; it has a thousand pockets, which keeps me organized; it's big enough for my music binder, which allows me to be hands-free when I sign in; and it's from Paris, France, which makes me feel fancy! ALL HAIL THE AUDITION BAG!

Here's what you should have in your bag:
   -Your audition binder
   This includes your sheet music, which is double-sided (for easy page turning for the pianist!) and clearly marked with your

intro and ending. It also has two copies of your headshot and resume, which are stapled back to back.

-Jazz shoes and character heels

It's MT baby! If you make it past the singing call, it's time for dancing! Even if it doesn't say to bring your dance shoes, BRING THEM. I can't count the times I've been asked to dance with no warning. (Cue me crying in the corner—before I remember to practice my positive self-talk!)

*Bonus points: if you're a tapper, add your tap shoes just in case.

-Pen and a highlighter

You're constantly filling out paperwork. Do yourself a solid and throw a couple in there. Plus, when you get callbacks or sides on the spot, you'll be so grateful to quickly be able to highlight your lines and make acting notes for yourself.

-Snacks

Throw in some protein bars, popcorn, crackers, whatever you fancy! MT calls and callbacks are notorious for lots of waiting around, and we're not at the top of our game if we're hungry... or HANGRY!

-Grether's Pastilles

This is not an ad, but I love these! They are the best singing lozenges around and keep your throat from feeling dry in weird AC or just from nerves.

-A Belt Box

This is not an ad either, and everyone makes me fun of me for it (I look hilarious using it), but when you've been waiting for a while, your voice cools down. Give the Belt Box a Google- it's a little mask you can sing into that dulls your sound so you won't annoy the people around you and can be vocally warm in the room!

7. You've checked traffic and directions.

You do not need anything to distract you from your audition the day of! So, at least the day before, check traffic and schedule when you'll leave! And, depending on where and when your appointment is, leave at least 15 to 60 minutes of margin! If it's a really important audition, you might even want to do a test-drive to scout out the location and parking to save yourself any unnecessary stress of being late!

8. You practiced your slate.

Last but not least, you've practiced your slate! This is always your name, and can be a few additional pieces of information: your agency, the role your auditioning for, your height, where you're based, if you have a valid passport, the song you're singing...

If it's an MT audition, state your name and the song you're singing. If it's Film/ TV, state your name, agency, and the role you're auditioning for.

If the CD wants any more specific of a slate, they'll let you know!

The funny thing about slating is that so many people joke about it being the hardest part! There's a tendency to feel robotic when saying your name, and it can throw you off! Make sure you smile and state your name clearly and distinctly.

So many of my students have a tendency to rush their name, which makes them sound nervous! Take control. Introduce yourself with confidence. Just like in your scene, remember that you're connecting with an actual person, even during your slate. You got this!

Do I really have to take Preparation THIS seriously ?

You've done it. You've packed your bag, checked WAZE, and you've memorized your material backward and forward, up and down.

But, just in case I haven't convinced you that preparation is the way, the truth, and the life...

Let's play "devil's advocate."

Why isn't it better to rock up and wing it with your charm and natural talent and swagger?

Because now you're leaving it all up to chance. You're relying on the fact that in the room, the pressure won't trip you up, that the good ideas and choices will just come to you, and that nobody will cough too loudly and the AC won't start *wheezing* and whirring halfway through your scene, etc.

Here's what's at stake without preparation:

If you're not memorized enough, you're chained to your sides. Now the audience/ casting has lost their connection to you. Eyes are the windows to the soul, right? If your eyes are glued to your script, how can we connect with you?

If you need to double-check if the line was "amazing" or "astonishing," you've suddenly needed to take your attention away from the reader, who is your scene partner. You're not thinking about how to get what you want anymore. You're thinking about the line. You are no longer listening to the intricacies of this stranger's delivery that will give you the clues of how to honestly respond. You're scrambling for what comes next. You can't be present when you're constantly playing catch up in the scene.

If you don't know what your character is fighting for in the scene, then I guarantee the scene will fall flat. Your audition will not be memorable (at least not in a good way), and this job will go to someone else.

What if you didn't bring snacks, and now the callback is going to last for the next five hours and you're already hungry?

There are so many unknown variables with every new audition. For me, it all comes down to this:

My most powerful way to fight my nerves is knowing that no matter what, I have done my absolute best with everything that is in my control. I have prepared my version of the material honestly and authentically. I've stretched my memorization skills, or dialect skills, or whatever the material required of me.

I've learned something new and practiced to the best of my ability. I know I'm a better actor today than I was yesterday.

With this knowledge, we can walk into the room knowing we have won because we are putting ourselves forward to the best of our abilities and now have the chance to show it off! To play! To listen! To explore! To have fun!

We cannot possibly book 100% of our auditions. But we can learn from 100% of our auditions.

When growing is the goal, when becoming more of the artist you dream of being today, than you were yesterday, is the measuring tape; then there is abundant freedom walking into the audition room.

You can walk in knowing you've won. You're sharing your passions and your preparation. You've done everything in your power to do your best.

Now, you're ready to own the audition room.

Affirmations:

I am as prepared as I can possibly be.

I am ready for this.

I can't wait to share what I've been working on.

4

Own the Casting Room During the Audition

My Favorite Audition EVER.

Do you know the magical story of "The Secret Garden," by Francis Hodgson Burnett? A total brat named Mary learns how to love and teaches a family to let go of the ghosts that haunt them while simultaneously bringing a secret garden back to life. It's a classic!

An award-winning company in LA I absolutely adored was holding auditions for The Secret Garden. Enter a multitude of butterflies in my stomach because I had always wanted to play the character of Martha, Mary's maid! Not only is Martha quirky, hilarious, and heartfelt (my JAM!), but she also gets the "eleven o'clock" ballad in act two that convinces the lead character, Mary, to "hold on!", and not give up hope. When done correctly, there's not a dry eye in the house. All signs point to... dream role!

But when I got the audition from my agent, I wasn't called in for Martha! I was called in for Rose, Mary's mother! Cue despair! Don't worry—I wasn't so easily dissuaded from my mission. I dutifully prepared the sides for Rose, but also focused on creating my absolute best version of the Martha sides (I traversed the internet until I found them! *The name is Bond. Renna Bond*).

The day of the audition arrived. I sang my heart out for the Rose sides and then asked, ever so politely, if I could "please read for Martha as well?" The team was generous and kind and gave me the thumb's up.

We began the scene.

It was truly one of the most magical moments of my artistic life. As I read the scenes, I felt what some people call being "in the flow." I experienced such laser beam focus and creativity, and sensed the energy of the room tuning into my every word.

In the acting world, we call this being "present."

I trusted the thorough preparation I'd done for the material and allowed my connection with the reader to guide the scene, which kept it honest and authentic. I made the team laugh, and more importantly, I made them listen.

I left the room knowing that I'd book that role. But, even more significantly, that during the magical two minutes of that scene, I had set my soul free from fear and nerves to be truly expressive, creative, and mostly, myself.

What a powerful, beautiful thing.

The Power of Presence

Much like in the world outside of entertainment, being present is what unlocks connection, opportunity, peace, and joy.

When is the last time you felt completely present? Where to-do lists did not shout at you from the corners of your brain? Or when you weren't trapped in wishing things were how they used to be? Or when you totally forgot about checking your phone because the conversation was spell-binding?

Who were you with? What did you do to anchor yourself to that moment?

We are able to be present most often with people we love, or are fascinated by. It's by trusting and listening to the other person that we are able to become the most present. This requires vulnerability to be open to slowing down, and open to connecting with someone else.

Most significantly, being present cannot be faked. We humans have an innate sense of knowing whether someone is actually listening, and actually engaged with us in a conversation.

What sorts of things keep you from being present?

My biggest hurdles to being present are three things:

1. Stress

2. Worrying about what just happened
3. Worrying about what will happen next

Stress clouds our vision with pressing things we need to get done, like never-ending to-do lists. Often, I'm stuck wondering if I've forgotten to do something! Does this sound familiar?

In the audition room, stress makes us worry about ourselves! Thoughts like these take up all the space in our brains:
 -Where should I stand?
 -Who is my reader?
 -Have I seen this casting team before?
 -Does the accompanist know this song?
 -Do I look ok?
 -What's my line?
 -Am I good enough?
 -Why did I wear these shoes?
 -Why did I pick this song?

Or, worrying about what just happened takes over like this:
 -Why did my slate sound so nervous?
 -Did I move my hands in a weird way?
 -I messed up that note!
 -Did I sound honest?
 -Did I blink too much?

And last but not least, worrying about what will happen next presents itself in these thoughts:
 -Are they going to ask me for another song?
 -Do I get to read both sides?
 -Am I going to have to dance after?

-Am I going to get a callback?
-Do I have time to get lunch before the callback?
-Will I have to call out of work if the callback runs late?
-Do I have enough money in the parking meter?
-Will I get this job?

Clearly, we cannot be present in our audition with the casting director, reader, and our material if this cacophony is competing for space in our heads!

So what do we do to quiet the stress, the worry of what just happened, and what will happen next?

We lean into the power of being present.

Before the Actual Audition

When Does Your Audition Start?

True or false: your audition starts when you walk into the casting room.

FALSE! Your audition starts when you get into the building! Why? We never know who is watching! I've been to two auditions where they've had a member of the casting team sit in the waiting area and literally take notes on how the people auditioning interact with each other. This may sound creepy or unfair, but it isn't! Being a kind person that others would want to work with is part of the job! One of my best friends has been an Equity monitor (the person running the sign in, lining people up, and bringing people into the casting room), and has been asked by casting about how certain actors were treating others. *Do not lose the gig because you're having a bad day and you snapped at someone else!* Also... just be a kind person.

Ok, now you're in the waiting room. You've signed in and been really respectful and friendly to the monitor and you're waiting to go in for your audition. Now what?

It's time to fight your nerves.

B. B. H.

Imagine this: there are three people ahead of you. You realize it's about time to go do the thing you've been prepping for and dreaming of! Your palms start to sweat. Your shoulders tense. Your heart races. What's going on?!

Your body thinks it's in danger. This is a primal response, but don't worry—here's how you handle it:

B. B. H.

The first "B" stands for "brain." Did you know fear and excitement produce the same chemicals in our brains? Read that again:

Fear and excitement produce the same chemicals in our brains.

That means we're in the driver's seat: we get to tell our brains if we are *afraid* or if we are *excited*! LIGHTBULB MOMENT!

Next time you feel those butterflies before your audition, tell them to get in formation, because you are EXCITED.

Say it with me: "These are excited butterflies."

We've tackled our brain, so now we can move on to the second "B" in "B. B. H.", which stands for body.

What we do here is deep breathing. Short breaths tell our brains that we're in big trouble, so remind your body that you *wanted* to be here with some nice, long, deep breaths. Pay attention to your shoulders, jaw, and neck, which are common places to hold tension. Give them a shake and remind yourself, "I am safe."

Who's ready for the final letter? Time for "H," which stands for "heart."

This is my favorite one! We get our hearts ready for auditions by connecting with the other people auditioning. Make a friend. Encourage someone. Compliment another's outfit. Ask how their day is. Sometimes, people are too nervous to want to chat, but most of the time, the other actors are so nervous, they're looking for a lifeline of kindness. Be that lifeline.

What happens here is that you make a connection with others. You are subconsciously reminding yourself that you have worth beyond what is going to happen in the audition room, which helps put things into perspective. You are a real person, with real thoughts and feelings, and you are making the world a better place, just by being here.

Plus, you're practicing being present. You're practicing not focusing on what might happen in that room. You're listening to your new friend. You're honing in on *them*. And, just like in our scenes, if we are so focused on our scene partner/ new friend, we're not worrying about ourselves.

Science tells us that kindness releases positive hormones (oxytocin) that can contribute to a positive mood and general wellness. Powerful, right?

And, as a minuscule bonus? Encouraging others and chatting with them keeps your voice warm for the audition.

Wait, Renna—you're telling me that being a kind human not only helps others, but also helps myself?

Why, yes, friend. Yes, I am. It's crazy what happens when we focus on lifting others up!

Before we move on, a final pro tip: do not tell yourself or others at the call that you're nervous. Your brain is exceptionally powerful and will manifest what you say (remember this from chapter one!). If you tell yourself that you're nervous, guess what? Your brain follows the command and helps you *be* nervous. As we learned, your language is important. Your new narrative is: "I'm excited!", which brings your brain on board!

The bottom line here is: you are in control of your thoughts, which are in control of your body.

Ok, now you're on deck to go into your audition! What do you do?

Final Systems Check!

Right before I go into my audition, I like to do three things:

1. Glance at my starting point of my sides.

I like to check my first phrase of my scene or song one more time, and remember where my character is coming from emotionally, so I'm ready to go when the CD asks me to begin!

2) Affirmations!

I hope you've been enjoying the affirmations at the end of each chapter! As we've discussed, affirmations are a powerful tool to rewire our brains to circulate and manifest new positive beliefs. Right before I go into the room, I love to say an affirmation or two to remind myself that I'm about to kick butt! Some that I enjoy using are:

-I am an artist.
  -I love to tell this story!
  -I can't wait to share what I've been working on!
  -I am ready and right for this!

Feel free to steal one of mine, or write your own! Think about what you most need to hear. Be the voice you need!

3) Pray!

For me, this is a moment to thank God for the opportunity of sharing my gifts and being creative, but this can look however you want! Pray, connect with the universe, thank someone in your heart. Our gratitude is infectious, and the perfect energy to bring into the room with us!

Ok, it's time! You're going in! Now what?

During the Actual Audition

The Day All My Auditions Changed

How do you walk into the audition room?

I used to peek my head in, tiptoe over to the piano and whisper my rhythm to the accompanist, and then shuffle to my mark in silence until the CD spoke to me. I was trying not to disturb anyone, and often when you walk in, the team is discussing the person before you. I was trying to be respectful.

But actually, I looked terrified. I looked like I had no confidence, and like I was apologizing for taking up space and time. I still booked like this, but let me tell you: in 2019, I made a New Year's resolution to be fearless in audition rooms. That applied to my material choices, my acting choices, my outfits, but most of all, it applied to the way I walked in.

As of January 1, 2019, GONE were the days of being mousy! *Adios* to sneaking in! "No, thank you!", to apologizing for existing! Now, when I enter the room, I take up space!

I basically shout, "Hey, everybody! How's it going?" I am beaming! I am relaxed. I am excited to share my favorite thing: storytelling. I listen to see if the CD wants to chat. I'm friendly with the pianist in my normal voice (no more hushed tones!).

I am not kidding: the second I started boldly entering rooms, my callback ratio literally doubled, and I booked one of my favorite jobs—being an international lead vocalist for Hong Kong Disneyland! I got to live in Asia for over a year, learn a new language, meet people from all over the world (including some of my very best friends!), and check off two dream roles, all while performing for a living and saving a ton of money!

Our takeaway here? TAKE UP SPACE! You deserve to be here! So act like it!

Let's put ourselves in the casting director's shoes. Would you want to hire someone bold and confident, or shy and apologetic? Also, you're probably going to be a human with empathy and feel nervous FOR the anxious auditioner! The second you put the casting director at ease, they can relax and focus on considering where you'd fit in their puzzle! *Badda bing, badda boom.*

So now you've entered the room like the rockstar that you are! You've greeted everyone in the room! Now, it's time to connect.

Connect

Auditions can feel like high-pressure situations, right? Well, they *did* before you learned about B. B. H! But, when we're in high-pressure circumstances, it can be difficult to remember that we're dealing with other humans.

Not only is your audition about you, but it's also about your casting director, your reader, your pianist, etc.

These are not just nameless powers that be. They're theatre/ movie nerds, just like you!

How do you like to be treated when you meet someone new? I'm a big fan when someone puts me at ease by asking how my day is going, or compliments my outfit. These are super basic rules of society, right? But the second we enter the audition room, we can forget how to be a human who's interacting with other humans!

So simply, start there. Ask everybody how they're doing, how they're enjoying your city if it's an audition tour, give them a compliment about being efficient or kind, or whatever you're experiencing. This shows the team that you see them as equals and collaborators; not as gods reaching down to you, a mere mortal!

It's also a step towards being present, which, as we've mentioned, is the magical key to enjoying yourself, being free and confident to do your best work, and in turn, makes them see why they'd want to cast you!

Now, you've connected! You've had a giggle with them, or discovered you both like the same band on the reader's T-shirt. You're human. You're ready.

The Material

You've been given the go-ahead to start your scene or song.

A huge mistake I see people making over and over, is diving immediately into starting.

Ninety-nine out of one hundred times, the way casting tells you to start is by saying, "Whenever you're ready."

They mean it. They're not being rude or sarcastic.

So, take a second. Think about your character, where you're coming from. Look at a spot on the wall above the casting director's head, and *see* the person you're talking to. What is your imaginary scene partner wearing? Or, if you're reading with a reader, notice the reader. What color eyes do they have?

Cuing in on these details keeps you present.

Then, when you really are ready, begin!

See it, Fight for it, Enjoy it

You've finally begun! You're doing it!

Your most important task during your reading/ singing is to stay present and connected with either your reader, or your imaginary scene partner. I tell this to all of my students because it is true one hundred percent of the time: if you see it, I see it. This applies to your scene partner, your surroundings, the thing you want.

YOU are the master of creating this reality and running with it. How fun is that? Remember when you used to play "make believe" as a kid? All those imagination skills you honed are your bread and butter now. How amazing is that?

You're seeing your scene partner, either real or imaginary! You're watching their expressions change as you listen to them and interact with them. Now, you have to convince them to give you what your character wants! Getting what we want is another skill that most people are generally good at. Doing the same thing over and over when trying to convince someone to give you something, is not going to give you a new result. But what will? Changing your tactics. Asking coyly didn't work? Ok, time to intimidate them! That didn't work? How about a little bribery?

Remember, you don't know how the scene is going to go. Sure—you, the actor, know how it's written. But your scene partner is going to make it different for you. Maybe you imagined the scene going really quietly and gently, but your reader is yelling at you! Time to adjust and meet them where they are! Or, maybe your scene partner makes you laugh. How would your character roll with that?

The worst thing you can do is play the scene as you imagined it going, and not tune into your scene partner. This is not called acting. This is what I call, *showing*. You're showing us a performance, instead of living authentically in the given circumstances. Not only will "showing" *not* get you the job, but it will also be way less fun.

Fighting for what you want and playing with your real or imaginary scene partner is where the joy and creativity and freshness is! So make sure you are truly enjoying it! You have worked so hard to prepare for this. You've memorized and you've created a character and you've practiced for coaches and friends. Now, live it up by trusting the work you've done and living in the moment by focusing on your partner.

Collaboration in the audition room, in coaching sessions, and onstage is the magic that keeps me coming back, and I want you feel the same way! It's an electric moment of connection and creativity with another person that reminds us, we are not alone, we have something to say, and we can say it beautifully together. Ok, let me grab a tissue!

Face It

You know that nanosecond after you finish the sides? When you know exactly how you feel it went, AKA good or bad?

If you wish it had gone better, here's what you will NEVER do again:

Show disappointment on your face.

There is nothing that shoots you in the foot faster than showing the team that you think you whiffed it, as my Nana would say.

A professional does their job, trusts their work, and then is on to the next one.

And so are you.

I do not care if you messed up every line. I do not care if you cracked louder than the Liberty Bell. I don't care if you tripped and literally face-planted. After the sides are done, you will smile, maintain confident posture, and await the direction of the casting team. Got it? NO EXCEPTIONS.

When they let you go, thank them warmly, and be on your merry way.

You just did it. You hacked the first two parts of your audition.

Affirmations

I was made for this.

I am present.

I am a storyteller.

5

Master Your Mindset After the Audition

So Now What?

You just completed your audition! Congratulations! Cue confetti and happy dancing! How are you feeling?

Likely, you're feeling a PLETHORA of emotions. Relief is one emotion you're feeling, right? Because regardless of how it went, it happened! It's no longer looming in your brain. Now your audition is out in the world!

Sadly, if you're like most of us actors, you're also experiencing a swirl of negative emotions. You may be judging yourself because your audition didn't go exactly as you hoped it would. Maybe you're comparing yourself because some people were asked to perform more material than you were.

But mostly, you're probably glued to your phone, obsessed with waiting for casting news! Every *ping* or *ding* on your device is the possibility of a "yes" to move forward!

The anticipation *before* the audition, the thrill *of* the actual audition, and the come down *from* the audition make up a wild rollercoaster.

So how do we process what happened in the room? We left our heart in there! We spent literally hours preparing, memorizing, choosing outfits, mapping traffic and reconfiguring our schedules to make it happen! And now... we wait?!

How do we not let the waiting feel like a medieval torture tool?

We master our mindset.

Mastering our Mindset

Step One: The Audition is the Job

I've got some breaking news for you. As actors, our job is to audition. Any bookings or performances are icing on the cake.

If you are measuring the success of your auditions by whether or not you book them, you will be setting yourself up for ongoing disappointment. I'm not trying to be negative or discouraging, but rather encouraging!

The numbers are against us. There are just not enough projects to host the amount of actors out there. Even if you are winning Oscars, you are not booking everything! Our queen, Meryl Streep, does not get to do every project she dreams of! And if it's happening to Meryl... the rest of us mortals aren't safe from rejection either!

So what do we do? How do we keep the "no's" from getting us down?

We change our focus to the audition.

From now on, the job you're auditioning *for* is not the main thing. The *audition* is the main thing. The audition is what you prepare for, look forward to, and enjoy! If we stop treating auditions as a means to an end, but rather an actual stop on our super rad road trip (say that five times fast!), we will be able to glean joy!

Here is how you measure your auditions:

1. *Was I prepared?*

-Did you feel comfortable and confident enough in your material that you weren't scrounging in your brain for words, lyrics, notes, and acting beats?
   -Did you bring a properly stapled headshot and resume if required?
   -Were you dressed appropriately to be able to deliver your best performance?
   -Were you on time?
   -Did you research the project to make sure you were as knowledgable about the project as possible?
   -Did you integrate what you'd learned from your previous auditions?

2. *Was I present?*

-Were you able to connect with your scene partner and fight for what your character wanted?

-Could you block out the unexpected situations and environment that could have distracted you?

-Were you listening to both the casting director and your reader/ scene partner?

-If you got distracted, did you quickly dive back into the moment to get back on track?

This is the part that is always most difficult for me! To this day, this is my biggest focus and the thing I strive most to achieve: to get out of my head and into the scene!

3. Was I pleasant?

-Did I brighten the day of the monitor, other auditioners, and casting team?

-Did I bring positive energy with me into the waiting and casting rooms, no matter what wild things were stressing me out before (traffic, my family needing something, spilling coffee on my carefully chosen audition 'fit)?

If you are honestly able to answer to all of those questions with a resounding "Yes!", then congratulations! Your audition literally could not have gone any better! You have done your best. You have nailed the things that were in your control! You worked your butt off before, showed up, and showed off! You literally cannot ask for more from yourself!

Your new goal is to find the satisfaction here: from your effort with the list above. Find your satisfaction from pouring your heart, mind, soul, energy, time, and resources into your opportunities. Because regardless of the outcome of this audition, for the time encompassing the audition process, you were making art. You got to share your creativity and your whole self with an audience (the casting team).

Can you find pride in yourself in this process? Are you able to celebrate your efforts and be your own cheerleader?

Not every audition will go well, even if you've prepared with the process in chapters one and two! The way to deal with this is by employing the mind game strategies from chapter one, learning from what went wrong, laughing a little, and moving forward.

So many people groan about auditions. They find them annoying, scary, time-consuming, and discouraging. To be honest with you, sometimes, they can be. But that's exactly why we are rewriting the narrative.

We are falling in love with our craft instead of worshipping results that are completely out of our control. We are choosing not to take umbrage with the process, but rather, igniting our imagination and choosing to see each opportunity as a way to stretch and strengthen our creative muscles.

In this way, we are not prisoners, but pioneers. Truly, our mindset makes all the difference! We have agency, we have choice, and we are at the helm of how we feel about ourselves.

Step Two: Let It Go

It's time to take a snowflake out of Elsa's blizzard and, "Let it go."

But, Renna, what's the point of letting it go?

I'm so glad you asked!

We're shifting our focus from goal-oriented to process-oriented, and measuring what we can control, which is the audition. I do not want you to obsess and stress about the "what happens next" portion of the process. Let it be a thrilling surprise if you hear back.

Waiting for a callback can often feel like you're in a hospital room, waiting to hear back on the state of a loved one's surgery. I know this is wildly dramatic, but go with me on this! You gave literal birth to a creative idea in your audition, and now, it's out of your hands! You don't know if your audition will survive to the next stage of life! So what do you do? Pace around all day, phone in hand, sweating, worrying, obsessing, eating cartons of ice cream, and judging your audition from a thousand different angles?! Absolutely not. This is not healthy or helpful behavior (except the ice cream thing—this, I totally support!).

This result-obsessive behavior stops now. Instead of pacing the metaphorical waiting room, here's what you're going to do:

Celebrate!

Once you've walked out of the building, it's done. Remember how the audition is the job? Now, the job is over. You're not waiting for a callback. You're not waiting for a booking. You did it. You completed the project, accomplished the mission.

Treat it like a mini graduation. You worked hard, you did your best, and now it's done! Time to celebrate!

Do not skip this step. What's something that delights you? It could be having your friends over for a movie night, taking your dog for a walk, stopping for your favorite treat on the way home, or listening to your favorite band. What we're doing here is fun, but it's also scientific! We are creating neural pathways in your brain that equate auditioning with good things!

Just like Pavlov's dog, you'll be stoked when you get the audition if you know something fun is going to follow it!

Keep Track

A fun way I like to celebrate is by keeping track of my auditions in my journal. I love to see the names of projects written down and remember what I learned from them and, often, funny or victorious audition stories associated with them!

Here's the secret: don't write your auditions down until you've done them. As in, don't write them down when you get them, or when you're working on them, but only after you auditioned. This act also helps reinforce that the audition was the main goal, and it's now a finished project.

Sides-Eye

Ok don't give me the side-eye for this one, but the minute you're out of the building, trash your sides! Don't keep them in case of a callback! Often, the callback sides are different anyway, so there's no point in keeping them! This is a metaphorical act of "washing your hands" from the audition. It's out of your life!

Step Three: Reflect

What Did You Learn?

You know how when you accomplish something great, or experience something awesome, you naturally reflect on it? You think things like:

"Can you believe I graduated?!"

"Weren't those stars ridiculously bright last night?"

"Holy cannoli, that meal had no business being that delicious!"

"Dang. That was a really great day."

"I'm really proud of how I handled that difficult conversation."

Auditions are no different. Now that we've closed the chapter on that particular audition, it's the perfect time to reflect on it. I like to journal right before I go to sleep. Here are some questions to ask yourself about the audition:

-What's something I did that I'm really proud of?

Did you enter the room with confidence? Did you have an

amazing conversation with the monitor in the waiting room? Did you land the character arc you planned? Or maybe you made the CD laugh with a choice you made?

-What would I do differently next time?

Maybe traffic was heavier than you expected, so you're going to add some more margin for travel time in the future. Or, maybe you realized your shirt felt a little distracting because it was too short/ too big/ etc so you won't wear it for auditions anymore. Or, next time, maybe you'll try to get back to the connection with your reader faster after a distraction.

-What did I enjoy most about that process?

Where did you feel joy? Was it in an "aha!" moment about your character while you were prepping? Was it meeting a kindred spirit in the audition room? Was it feeling free and grounded in the room? Or the fact that you showed up and faced any nerves head-on?

Your growth as an artist and as a human is one of the main reasons you were put on this earth, and this is a tangible way to help you process, implement, and celebrate that growth!

Step Four: The Longterm Game

Can I tell you about my last audition? I got to bring in my own 16-bar-cut, so I chose a song I am LOVING right now. I've mastered all of the trouble spots, connected with the lyrics, and now I am truly stoked whenever I get to sing it.

I walked in prepped. I walked in confident. I had a lovely chat with the monitor, who told me they were giving out callbacks in the room. My outfit was a ten out of ten! I was ready to rock!

When they called me in, I owed the room. I connected with the pianist and the CD. And then, dear reader, I gave the best rendition of that song I have ever done. I was grounded. My voice was free. The story was front and center. I had an arc! I had layers! And my voice was in top form! I smashed it! I was ready for my callback!

I grinned expectantly. But then, "Thank you."

"Thank you," as in, a dismissal. As in, no callback. I was crushed. This audition felt harder to leave behind because I was so proud of the work that I'd done in the room, and I'd focused too much on the callback, rather than the audition itself.

I was processing this with my incredible coach, and she said that I have to play the long-term game. "What you did today was make a fan out of that casting director," she said. "They saw you at your best, and they'll remember you in the future. You probably didn't get called back because the role you were right for was already cast, or you were the wrong physical type. Whatever it was, it was out of your control. You didn't go to that audition for *this* job. You went to that audition for the next fifty jobs!"

Can you see why she's my favorite coach? I mean, what words of wisdom! Mic drop!

She's right: we're not just auditioning for the project that we go in for on audition day. We're auditioning for anything that this casting director is working on now, or in the future!

Let this give you hope and solace when you don't hear back. It's not a "no." It's a "not yet."

Hilariously, right after she encouraged me with this pep talk, I was brought in straight to callbacks for a different project by the same casting director (I even had to sign an "NDA" to get the script because it was so high-profile! Sometimes auditions are fun that way)! She was 100% right—it wasn't just one great audition. It was an audition to get me in the door for the next project!

Affirmations:

Some helpful post-audition mindsets I employ through affirmations:

-This is my choice.

When I'm feeling frustrated by not getting a callback or booking, I like to remember that it was my choice to say "yes" to this opportunity, and that it's my choice to keep going in this career path. I'm not on a hamster wheel trying to people-please the powers that be. I'm an artist choosing to find delight in the challenge and pride in watching myself grow in tenacity and perseverance.

-The right project is on its way to me.

As an actor, your entire day can change with an email, and your entire life can change with a call. We can't predict when these emails or calls come to us. With the right attitude, this can be an exciting thought to lead you through the day and keep you excited for what's to come! You never know when the next big thing will land in your hands, so stay ready for it by keeping on top of your skills.

–I'm proud of the work I've done and excited to see how I grow in the future.

I cannot impress upon you enough how important it is to celebrate the work you've done. You cannot move forward with pride and confidence if you don't take time to revel in your growth! It should excite you to continue on your path to being the artist and human you were always meant to be.

6

Go Get 'Em

You've got this.

You showed up for your dream by reading this book! That is 100% worth celebrating! You are equipped to thrive in your upcoming auditions!

You now know how to:

1. Fight the battle before the audition with fool-proof preparation! You know that diving into the process of preparing provides you freedom in the room. It alleviates your fears and enables you to walk in confidently because you are thrilled to share what you've worked on.

1. Own the audition room! You're going to take up space, connect with the other humans in the room and spend your

performing portion fighting for what your character wants by being present with your real or imagined scene partner!

1. Master your mindset! You will no longer measure your success by things that are outside of your control, like callbacks and bookings. You are going to celebrate your hard work, learn from your experience, and play the long-term game!

And because I want to help you succeed in incorporating what you've learned, please enjoy A full list of affirmations from each chapter, an audition packing checklist, and an audition journal, that follow! If you have questions, comments, or are interested in coaching sessions, please email me at renna.nightingale@gmail.com.

If this book empowered you or made you smile, I'd be honored (and grateful!) if you left a favorable review on Amazon!

May you be led by imagination, hope, and wonder. Choosing to persevere with passion and joy in a field rife with obstacles and rejection is our boldest form of rebellion.

7

Epilogue: Inciting Incident

At the beginning of every hero's journey, there's an inciting incident: something where the hero has to choose to either stay the same, or start down the path that will change everything.

Would you want to watch a movie about someone who chose not to take the adventure? Who chose to retreat instead of fight? Or chose to stay the same instead of grow?

No, you wouldn't.

Let this book be your inciting incident.

Use the tools laid out for you. Take time to process which thought-patterns are keeping you from walking in fearlessness and presence. Choose to be bold and committed in your preparation. Take charge of your body and mind with B.B.H. to fight your fears and also make the world a kinder place. Live in the thrill of storytelling. And then, let it go. Create an audition cycle that inspires you, empowers you, and sets you free.

You are the hero of your own story. It's up to you: will you stay the same, or will you begin your hero's journey?

The choice is yours.

8

Full List of Affirmations

- I am enough.
- I am here for a reason.
- I can figure anything out.
- I am capable.
- I am powerful.
- I am radiant.
- I am resilient.
- I am an artist.
- I am free and safe to create.
- I love myself for who I am.
- I was made for this.
- I deserve to chase my dreams.
- I am focused.
- I am prepared.
- I am ready.
- I am excited.
- I am as prepared as I can possibly be.
- I am ready for this.

- I can't wait to share what I've been working on.
- I am present.
- I am a storyteller.
- I deserve to take up space.
- This is my choice.
- The right project is on its way to me.
- I'm proud of the work I've done and excited to see how I grow in the future.
- This is my hero's journey.

9

Audition Packing List

Film/ TV Auditions:

- Sides
- Headshot and resumé
- Water
- A snack
- Chapstick

Musical Theatre Auditions:

- Audition Book
- Sides
- Headshot and resumé
- Character shoes
- Jazz shoes
- Tap shoes
- Pen
- Highlighter

- Water (TONS OF WATER. LIKE AN OCEAN OF WATER.)
- Snacks
- Grether's Pastilles (optional)
- Belt Box (optional)

10

Audition Journal

Audition Journal

Project Name: _____

1. Was I prepared?

Yes/ No: Did you feel comfortable and confident enough in your material?
Yes/ No: Did you have everything you needed?
Yes/ No: Were you on time?

2. Was I present?

Yes/ No: Did you connect with your scene partner and fight for what your character wanted?
Yes/ No: Were you able to block out distractions?
Yes/ No: If you got distracted, did you dive back into the moment to get back on track?

3. Was I pleasant?

Yes/ No: Did I brighten the day of the monitor, other auditioners, and casting team?
Yes/ No: Did I bring positive energy with me into the waiting and casting rooms?

What's something I did that I'm really proud of?

_____
_____
_____
_____

What's something I would do differently next time?

_____
_____
_____

What did I enjoy most about that process?

_____
_____
_____
_____

Affirmation that helped me most: _____

AUDITION JOURNAL

Audition Journal

Project Name: _____

1. *Was I prepared?*

Yes/ No: Did you feel comfortable and confident enough in your material?
Yes/ No: Did you have everything you needed?
Yes/ No: Were you on time?

2. *Was I present?*

Yes/ No: Did you connect with your scene partner and fight for what your character wanted?
Yes/ No: Were you able to block out distractions?
Yes/ No: If you got distracted, did you dive back into the moment to get back on track?

3. *Was I pleasant?*

Yes/ No: Did I brighten the day of the monitor, other auditioners, and casting team?
Yes/ No: Did I bring positive energy with me into the waiting and casting rooms?

What's something I did that I'm really proud of?

_____
_____
_____
_____

What's something I would do differently next time?

_____
_____
_____

What did I enjoy most about that process?

_____
_____
_____
_____

Affirmation that helped me most: _____

Audition Journal

Project Name: _____

1. Was I prepared?

Yes/ No: Did you feel comfortable and confident enough in your material?
Yes/ No: Did you have everything you needed?
Yes/ No: Were you on time?

2. Was I present?

Yes/ No: Did you connect with your scene partner and fight for what your character wanted?
Yes/ No: Were you able to block out distractions?
Yes/ No: If you got distracted, did you dive back into the moment to get back on track?

3. Was I pleasant?

Yes/ No: Did I brighten the day of the monitor, other auditioners, and casting team?
Yes/ No: Did I bring positive energy with me into the waiting and casting rooms?

What's something I did that I'm really proud of?

_____
_____
_____
_____

What's something I would do differently next time?

_____
_____
_____

What did I enjoy most about that process?

_____
_____
_____
_____

Affirmation that helped me most: _____

Audition Journal

Project Name: _____

1. *Was I prepared?*

Yes/ No: Did you feel comfortable and confident enough in your material?
Yes/ No: Did you have everything you needed?
Yes/ No: Were you on time?

2. *Was I present?*

Yes/ No: Did you connect with your scene partner and fight for what your character wanted?
Yes/ No: Were you able to block out distractions?
Yes/ No: If you got distracted, did you dive back into the moment to get back on track?

3. *Was I pleasant?*

Yes/ No: Did I brighten the day of the monitor, other auditioners, and casting team?
Yes/ No: Did I bring positive energy with me into the waiting and casting rooms?

What's something I did that I'm really proud of?

_____
_____
_____
_____

What's something I would do differently next time?

_____
_____
_____

What did I enjoy most about that process?

_____
_____
_____
_____

Affirmation that helped me most: _____

Audition Journal

Project Name: _____

1. *Was I prepared?*

Yes/ No: Did you feel comfortable and confident enough in your material?
Yes/ No: Did you have everything you needed?
Yes/ No: Were you on time?

2. *Was I present?*

Yes/ No: Did you connect with your scene partner and fight for what your character wanted?
Yes/ No: Were you able to block out distractions?
Yes/ No: If you got distracted, did you dive back into the moment to get back on track?

3. *Was I pleasant?*

Yes/ No: Did I brighten the day of the monitor, other auditioners, and casting team?
Yes/ No: Did I bring positive energy with me into the waiting and casting rooms?

What's something I did that I'm really proud of?

_____
_____
_____
_____

What's something I would do differently next time?

_____
_____
_____

What did I enjoy most about that process?

_____
_____
_____
_____

Affirmation that helped me most: _____

74

Audition Journal

Project Name: _____

1. *Was I prepared?*

Yes/ No: Did you feel comfortable and confident enough in your material?
Yes/ No: Did you have everything you needed?
Yes/ No: Were you on time?

2. *Was I present?*

Yes/ No: Did you connect with your scene partner and fight for what your character wanted?
Yes/ No: Were you able to block out distractions?
Yes/ No: If you got distracted, did you dive back into the moment to get back on track?

3. *Was I pleasant?*

Yes/ No: Did I brighten the day of the monitor, other auditioners, and casting team?
Yes/ No: Did I bring positive energy with me into the waiting and casting rooms?

What's something I did that I'm really proud of?

_____
_____
_____
_____

What's something I would do differently next time?

_____
_____
_____

What did I enjoy most about that process?

_____
_____
_____
_____

Affirmation that helped me most: _____

Audition Journal

Project Name: _____

1. *Was I prepared?*

Yes/ No: Did you feel comfortable and confident enough in your material?
Yes/ No: Did you have everything you needed?
Yes/ No: Were you on time?

2. Was I present?

Yes/ No: Did you connect with your scene partner and fight for what your character wanted?
Yes/ No: Were you able to block out distractions?
Yes/ No: If you got distracted, did you dive back into the moment to get back on track?

3. Was I pleasant?

Yes/ No: Did I brighten the day of the monitor, other auditioners, and casting team?
Yes/ No: Did I bring positive energy with me into the waiting and casting rooms?

What's something I did that I'm really proud of?

_____
_____
_____
_____

What's something I would do differently next time?

_____
_____
_____

What did I enjoy most about that process?

_____
_____
_____
_____

Affirmation that helped me most: _____

Audition Journal

Project Name: _____

1. Was I prepared?

Yes/ No: Did you feel comfortable and confident enough in your material?
Yes/ No: Did you have everything you needed?
Yes/ No: Were you on time?

2. Was I present?

Yes/ No: Did you connect with your scene partner and fight for what your character wanted?
Yes/ No: Were you able to block out distractions?
Yes/ No: If you got distracted, did you dive back into the moment to get back on track?

3. Was I pleasant?

Yes/ No: Did I brighten the day of the monitor, other auditioners, and casting team?
Yes/ No: Did I bring positive energy with me into the waiting and casting rooms?

What's something I did that I'm really proud of?

_____
_____
_____
_____

What's something I would do differently next time?

_____
_____
_____

What did I enjoy most about that process?

_____
_____
_____
_____

Affirmation that helped me most: _____

Audition Journal

Project Name: _____

1. *Was I prepared?*

Yes/ No: Did you feel comfortable and confident enough in your material?
Yes/ No: Did you have everything you needed?
Yes/ No: Were you on time?

2. *Was I present?*

Yes/ No: Did you connect with your scene partner and fight for what your character wanted?
Yes/ No: Were you able to block out distractions?
Yes/ No: If you got distracted, did you dive back into the moment to get back on track?

3. *Was I pleasant?*

Yes/ No: Did I brighten the day of the monitor, other auditioners, and casting team?
Yes/ No: Did I bring positive energy with me into the waiting and casting rooms?

What's something I did that I'm really proud of?

_____
_____
_____
_____

What's something I would do differently next time?

_____
_____
_____

What did I enjoy most about that process?

_____
_____
_____
_____

Affirmation that helped me most: _____

Audition Journal

Project Name: _____

1. *Was I prepared?*

Yes/ No: Did you feel comfortable and confident enough in your material?
Yes/ No: Did you have everything you needed?
Yes/ No: Were you on time?

2. *Was I present?*

Yes/ No: Did you connect with your scene partner and fight for what your character wanted?
Yes/ No: Were you able to block out distractions?
Yes/ No: If you got distracted, did you dive back into the moment to get back on track?

3. *Was I pleasant?*

Yes/ No: Did I brighten the day of the monitor, other auditioners, and casting team?
Yes/ No: Did I bring positive energy with me into the waiting and casting rooms?

What's something I did that I'm really proud of?

_____
_____
_____
_____

What's something I would do differently next time?

_____
_____
_____

What did I enjoy most about that process?

_____
_____
_____
_____

Affirmation that helped me most: _____

Audition Journal

Project Name: _____

1. Was I prepared?

Yes/ No: Did you feel comfortable and confident enough in your material?
Yes/ No: Did you have everything you needed?
Yes/ No: Were you on time?

2. Was I present?

Yes/ No: Did you connect with your scene partner and fight for what your character wanted?
Yes/ No: Were you able to block out distractions?
Yes/ No: If you got distracted, did you dive back into the moment to get back on track?

3. Was I pleasant?

Yes/ No: Did I brighten the day of the monitor, other auditioners, and casting team?
Yes/ No: Did I bring positive energy with me into the waiting and casting rooms?

What's something I did that I'm really proud of?

_____
_____
_____
_____

What's something I would do differently next time?

_____
_____
_____

What did I enjoy most about that process?

_____
_____
_____
_____

Affirmation that helped me most: _____

Audition Journal

Project Name: _____

1. *Was I prepared?*

Yes/ No: Did you feel comfortable and confident enough in your material?
Yes/ No: Did you have everything you needed?
Yes/ No: Were you on time?

2. *Was I present?*

Yes/ No: Did you connect with your scene partner and fight for what your character wanted?
Yes/ No: Were you able to block out distractions?
Yes/ No: If you got distracted, did you dive back into the moment to get back on track?

3. *Was I pleasant?*

Yes/ No: Did I brighten the day of the monitor, other auditioners, and casting team?
Yes/ No: Did I bring positive energy with me into the waiting and casting rooms?

What's something I did that I'm really proud of?

_____
_____
_____
_____

What's something I would do differently next time?

_____
_____
_____

What did I enjoy most about that process?

_____
_____
_____
_____

Affirmation that helped me most: _____

Audition Journal

Project Name: _____

1. *Was I prepared?*

Yes/ No: Did you feel comfortable and confident enough in your material?
Yes/ No: Did you have everything you needed?
Yes/ No: Were you on time?

2. *Was I present?*

Yes/ No: Did you connect with your scene partner and fight for what your character wanted?
Yes/ No: Were you able to block out distractions?
Yes/ No: If you got distracted, did you dive back into the moment to get back on track?

3. *Was I pleasant?*

Yes/ No: Did I brighten the day of the monitor, other auditioners, and casting team?
Yes/ No: Did I bring positive energy with me into the waiting and casting rooms?

What's something I did that I'm really proud of?

_____
_____
_____
_____

What's something I would do differently next time?

_____
_____
_____

What did I enjoy most about that process?

_____
_____
_____
_____

Affirmation that helped me most: _____

Audition Journal

Project Name: _____

1. *Was I prepared?*

Yes/ No: Did you feel comfortable and confident enough in your material?
Yes/ No: Did you have everything you needed?
Yes/ No: Were you on time?

2. *Was I present?*

Yes/ No: Did you connect with your scene partner and fight for what your character wanted?
Yes/ No: Were you able to block out distractions?
Yes/ No: If you got distracted, did you dive back into the moment to get back on track?

3. *Was I pleasant?*

Yes/ No: Did I brighten the day of the monitor, other auditioners, and casting team?
Yes/ No: Did I bring positive energy with me into the waiting and casting rooms?

What's something I did that I'm really proud of?

_____
_____
_____
_____

What's something I would do differently next time?

_____
_____
_____

What did I enjoy most about that process?

_____
_____
_____
_____

Affirmation that helped me most: _____

Audition Journal

Project Name: _____

1. *Was I prepared?*

Yes/ No: Did you feel comfortable and confident enough in your material?
Yes/ No: Did you have everything you needed?
Yes/ No: Were you on time?

2. *Was I present?*

Yes/ No: Did you connect with your scene partner and fight for what your character wanted?
Yes/ No: Were you able to block out distractions?
Yes/ No: If you got distracted, did you dive back into the moment to get back on track?

3. *Was I pleasant?*

Yes/ No: Did I brighten the day of the monitor, other auditioners, and casting team?
Yes/ No: Did I bring positive energy with me into the waiting and casting rooms?

What's something I did that I'm really proud of?

_____

_____

_____

_____

What's something I would do differently next time?

_____

_____

_____

What did I enjoy most about that process?

_____

_____

_____

_____

Affirmation that helped me most: _____

About the Author

Renna Nightingale is, above all things, a story-lover. She loves to read them, write them, perform in them, tell them, and watch them. She believes in the power of art to tell truths, transform, and heal. When she's offstage or off-camera, you can find her plotting her next travel adventure, pondering Impressionism in art museums, snuggling her rescue pup, or hunting down a cozy coffee shop. Psalm 34. @rennaissance on Instagram!

You can connect with me on:
🌐 https://rennanightingalehq.com

Subscribe to my newsletter:
✉ https://rennanightingalehq.com/jointheparty

Made in the USA
Columbia, SC
02 January 2025

51025052R00050